OTHER BOOKS IN THIS SERIES:
For a wonderful Mother A book to make your own
For a real Friend A book to make your own
A Girl's Journal A personal notebook and keepsake
A Woman's Journal A personal notebook and keepsake
Cats A book to make your own
Teddy Bears A book to make your own
Inspirations A book to make your own
A Gardener's Journal A book to make your own
OTHER HELEN EXLEY GIFTBOOKS
FOR GRANDMOTHERS:
The Love Between Grandparents and Grandchildren
To a very special Grandmother
To the World's best Grandmother (a book by kids)
A Little Book for my Grandma

Published in hardback 1990. Published in softcover 2001.
Copyright © Helen Exley 1990, 2001
Selection © Helen Exley 1990, 2001
Illustrations © Helen Exley 1990, 2001
The moral right of the author has been asserted.

12 11 10 9 8 7 6 5

ISBN 1-86187-216-X

Selection and design by Helen Exley
Illustrated by Juliette Clarke
Printed in China

Helen Exley Giftbooks, 16 Chalk Hill, Watford, Herts WD19 4BG, UK.
Helen Exley Giftbooks LLC, 185 Main Street, Spencer, MA 01562, USA.
www.helenexleygiftbooks.com

Acknowledgements: The publishers are grateful for permission to reproduce copyright material. Whilst every
reasonable effort has been made to trace copyright holders, we would be pleased to hear from any not here
acknowledged. Leonard Clark: "Cowslips" from *Collected Poems and Verses For Children*. Used by
permission of Dobson Books Ltd. Henry McMahan: "What is a Grandmother" from *Grandma was Quite a Girl* by
Harry and Gloria McMahan, Escondito, California. Charles and Ann Morse: From "Let this be a day for
Grandparents". Used by permission of Ann Morse. ROSANNE AMBROSE-BROWN; PAM BROWN; MARION C.
GARRETTY; CHARLOTTE GRAY; CLARA ORTEGA: published with permission © Helen Exley 1990, 2001.

For a wonderful

Grandmother

A BOOK TO MAKE YOUR OWN

A HELEN EXLEY
GIFTBOOK

𝒯hose gasps of astonishment, those shrieks of pleasure, those sighs of delight, lost long ago when your children grew wise and worldly, are suddenly given back to you by your grandchildren. What seem to be the same small hands clutch yours, dragging you from one excitement to another – "Look! Oh look! Come <u>On!</u>"

PAM BROWN

Ladies Smock.

.Primrose.

.Snowdrop.

.Violet.

Once a child is born, it is no longer in our power
not to love it nor care about it.

EPICTETUS

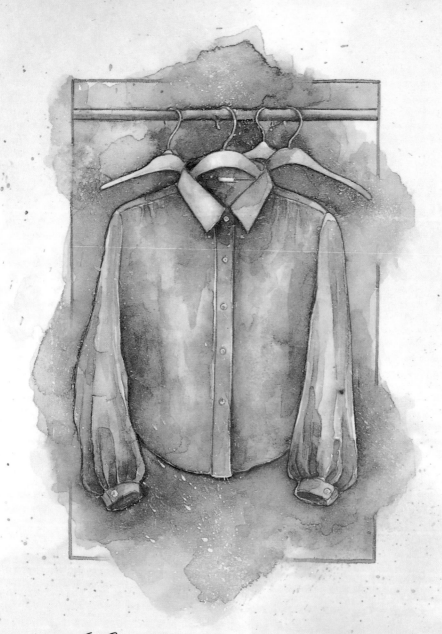

$\mathscr{G}$randmas are <u>always</u> astonished
to find themselves old enough to be grandmas.

JULIE B. JONES

*Our grandchildren accept us for ourselves, without rebuke
or effort to change us, as no one in our entire lives has ever done,
not our parents, siblings, spouses, friends –
and hardly ever our grown children.*

RUTH GOODE

Having grandchildren is the best of all possible worlds. I don't have any responsibility for them – I just do all the fun stuff.

MARY BETH

If anyone had told me I'd be sitting here on a coconut mat, waiting to slide down the helter skelter, I would have said....

MARION C. GARRETTY

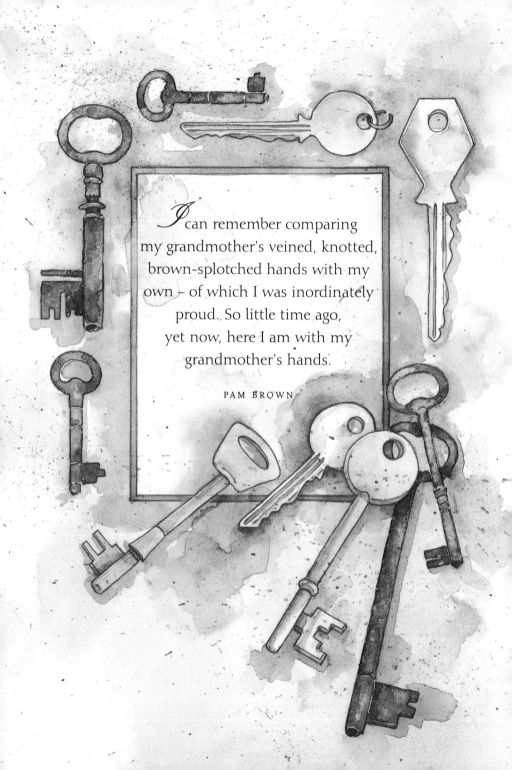

I can remember comparing
my grandmother's veined, knotted,
brown-splotched hands with my
own – of which I was inordinately
proud. So little time ago,
yet now, here I am with my
grandmother's hands.

PAM BROWN

There's something engaging
about the combination
of very young people and very mature people.
A child challenges most parents
to be stable and responsible.
A grandchild challenges the grandparent
to put aside all that stuff
and have fun.

CHARLES AND ANN MORSE

𝒯here are Respectable Grandmothers
and Undignified Grandmothers. The latter are far more fun.

EVA AND WILHELM KUPER

Grans take you on the really fast rides
at the fairground – even if they do go a very funny green.

JANE SWAN

Grandmas don't mind mud at all – not <u>proper</u> grans.

J.R. COULSON

Grandmothers are inclined to bring their grandchildren home muddy, sticky, radiant, exhausted and two hours late. Wise mothers say <u>nothing</u>.

CLARA ORTEGA

GRANDMOTHERS HAVE THE TIME

THEY NEVER HAD AS MOTHERS

– TIME TO TELL STORIES, TIME TO HEAR SECRETS,

TIME FOR CUDDLES.

DR. M. DE VRIES

One day we think, at last,
we have escaped the ties of children,
their troubles and their demands.
And then we feel a little tug – and find
ourselves bound, once more, by the
needs of our grandchildren.
And their love.

PAM BROWN

Grandparents are to be thanked for changing a child's fear of old age into a thing of strange beauty. It happens with the grandparent who gives a child tasty things to eat or who shows the child old and worn treasures or who knows how to touch a child as he awakens. Grandparents are to be thanked for showing a child, at the beginning of life, the gentleness of the end of life.

CHARLES AND ANN MORSE

What is a Grandmother?

Grandmothers don't have to do anything but be there. They are old so they shouldn't play hard or run. They should never say, "Hurry up". Usually they are fat, but not too fat to tie children's shoes. They wear glasses and funny underwear... they don't talk baby-talk like visitors. When they read to us, they don't skip bits, or mind if it is the same story over again. Everybody should have one... because grandmothers are the only grown-ups who have the time!

PATSY GRAY, AGE 7 ½

You should not be lulled
into a false sense of security
by knowing that you are
her grandchild.
Even grandmothers
can be Driven Too Far.

ROSANNE AMBROSE-BROWN

My grandmother is very patient.
She would have to
be with me around!

HELENA LEESON AGE 10

Grannys are dearly loved
by everyone. When your mother
tells you you are going to spend
a day or two at your granny's
you can't wait. When you fall over
and cut yourself mummy and
daddy are always too busy to put
a plaster on. So the only person
who is not too busy is granny.
At night time grannys
tuck you up in bed and make you
nice and snug.

JANE HIBBS AGE 9

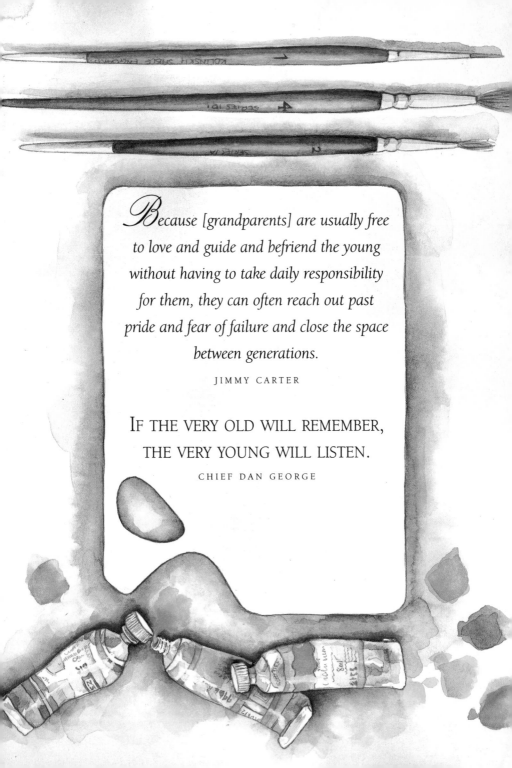

*Because [grandparents] are usually free
to love and guide and befriend the young
without having to take daily responsibility
for them, they can often reach out past
pride and fear of failure and close the space
between generations.*

JIMMY CARTER

IF THE VERY OLD WILL REMEMBER,
THE VERY YOUNG WILL LISTEN.

CHIEF DAN GEORGE

There are two lasting
bequests we can give
our children.
One of these is roots;
the other, wings.

HODDING CARTER

Grandmothers walk slowly
and so rediscover oil rainbows,
fallen leaves, puddles and worms
in need of rescue.

JULIE B. JONES

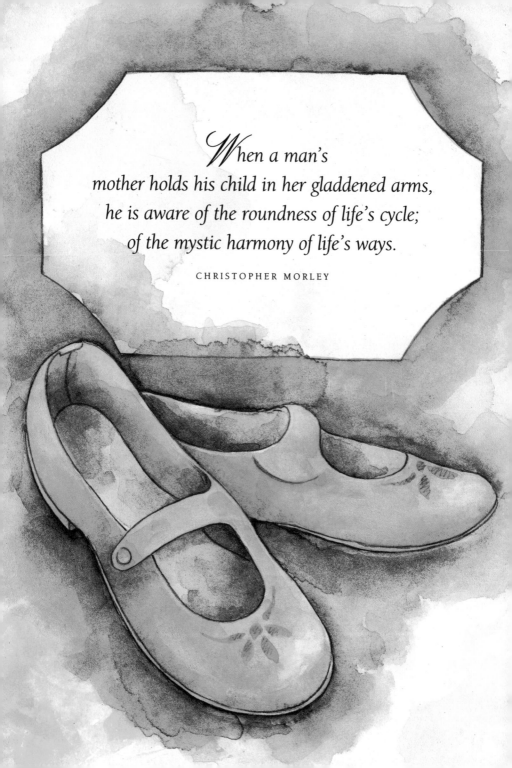

*When a man's
mother holds his child in her gladdened arms,
he is aware of the roundness of life's cycle;
of the mystic harmony of life's ways.*

CHRISTOPHER MORLEY

*S*ome grandma's smell of lavender soap, some grandmas smell of French perfume. My grandma smells of pastry and new bread and peppermints. My grandma smells gorgeous.

PETER

My grandmother

makes lots of cakes,

but the nicest thing about that is

she lets me

put the decorations

on the top.

TANYA BURCH AGE 9½

$\mathcal{A}$ faint aroma of gingerbread and all good
things mixed together seems to linger
all round a grandmother.

ELSPETH GORDON AGE 12

My nanna lets me lick the cake mixture when
she is finished. She lets me leave my food,
and she spoils me so much that when I grow
up I won't want anything.

SANDRA WEBB AGE 10

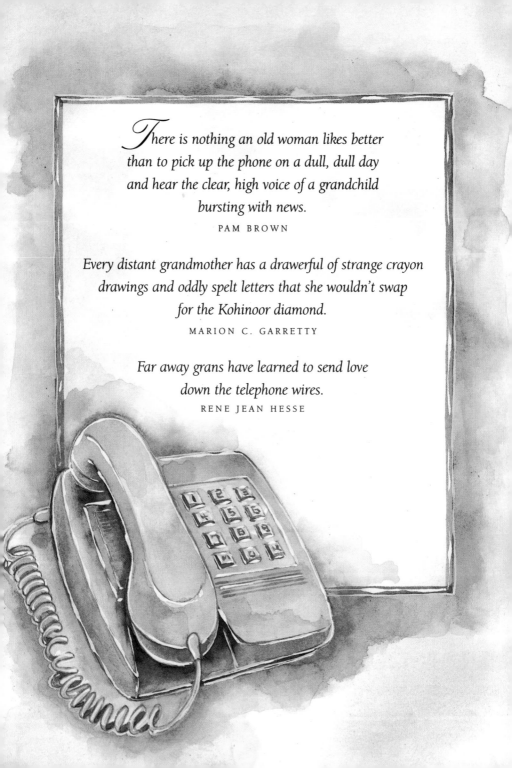

*There is nothing an old woman likes better
than to pick up the phone on a dull, dull day
and hear the clear, high voice of a grandchild
bursting with news.*

PAM BROWN

*Every distant grandmother has a drawerful of strange crayon
drawings and oddly spelt letters that she wouldn't swap
for the Kohinoor diamond.*

MARION C. GARRETTY

*Far away grans have learned to send love
down the telephone wires.*

RENE JEAN HESSE

After primroses, cowslips;

I like the name.

Born overnight in open fields

with new grass, first buttercups;

friends of the clay, they have a secret look.

Their heads catch the sun's gold,

dew pearls roll among crinkled leaves,

bees dust probing tongues in honeyed tubes.

My grandmother loved these flowers,

her mother, too, with the long apron strings,

gathered bunches in these same fields

for winter wine, syrups and creams;

I inherit them now, pick a hundred at a time,

make them into tight balls, as they did,

cowslip balls to hang about the thatched house,

smelling of orange and lemon,

pomanders in spring.

LEONARD CLARK

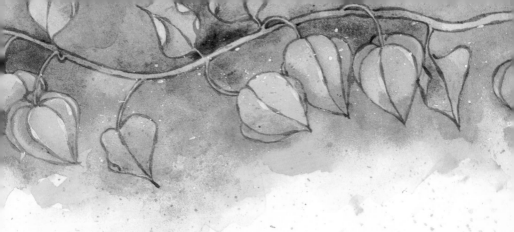

WHAT IS A GRANDMOTHER?

A grandmother is a little girl who suddenly shows up
one day with a touch of grey in her hair....

Long before Band-Aids were invented, she was the best
person to take care of scraped knees and scratched elbows
and banged heads. It was something in the way she
touched you.

Grandmother was an expert on mischief, too. Especially
when you had been into it. When she looked right into
your eyes it was pretty hard to fool her about what really
happened. Really.

And it was when you were almost too big to sit in her
lap that you began to learn that she was a very special
person to talk to. Sometimes, she would give you the right
answers without ever saying a word.

How did a little girl ever grow up to be so clever? Maybe
it came with the silver hair.

Maybe it came suddenly with being a grandmother.

HARRY McMAHAN

*Grandmother and grandchild discussing a common
interest are exactly the same age.*

DUANE BIRCH

THERE IS A FRISSON THAT COMES
WHEN A SMALL GRANDCHILD
SMILES UP INTO YOUR FACE AND SAYS
"OH, THANK YOU FOR BRINGING ME HERE",
EXACTLY AS HER MOTHER SAID
TWENTY YEARS BEFORE.

MONIQUE

*M*y grandmother is a refuge.
She is a gentle "relic" of the past (although I don't
think she would like me calling her that).
She is part of the past it is nice to think she has
journeyed through the years and is still so sensible
and kind. They take care of us, in loving us,
but ask for nothing in return.

SUSAN PHILPOT

Grandmas never notice that they have become old until their grandchildren subject them to a detailed examination. Having carefully noted wrinkles, whiskers, brown blotches, silver hair, blue veins and drooping jowls, they comment, with great kindness; "You're <u>very</u> old, aren't you, grandma?".

When, of course, it's time at last to admit it.

PAM BROWN

We all know grandparents whose values
transcend passing fads and pressures, and
who possess the wisdom of distilled pain and joy.

JIMMY CARTER

You can get a lot of extra mileage
out of a grandmother
if you let her have a cup of tea.

CHARLOTTE GRAY

Juliette Clarke
1990

*U*pstretched arms make grandmas
put off rheumatism till tomorrow.

JULIE B. JONES

WE ARE "JUST MUM" TO OUR
CHILDREN. TO OUR GRANDCHILDREN
WE ARE POSSESSED OF MAGIC....

M. C. G.

A grandma is old on the outside and young on the inside.

JOHN WRIGHT AGE 7½

Grandmas should write down the stories

of their lives, however dull they seem to them.

For such tales show history as it is —

a procession of interlocking lives. A unity.

The family of mankind.

CHARLOTTE GRAY

*M*others, flustered, busy, distracted,
inadvertently bring sorrow to their children.
Grandmothers have had time to look back and see
their own blunders clearly – and now they watch
their children making the same,
sad mistakes. All they can do is make a refuge
in their hearts where a grandchild
can find breathing space and comfort.

PAM BROWN

*Grandma simply never noticed
dress or status or skin.
She did not choose to ignore
such issues out of religious
or political conviction.
She just didn't notice them.
She only saw the individual.
It was her best legacy.*

CHARLOTTE GRAY

She has a past of her own
and a future which belongs
to everyone.
... she is a person who will
always have time to see you
when the rest of the world
is busy.

GILL WEBB